Charles Rogers

The Scottish House of Roger

With notes respecting the families of Playfair and Haldane of Bermony

I0692616

Charles Rogers

The Scottish House of Roger
With notes respecting the families of Playfair and Haldane of Bermony

ISBN/EAN: 9783337243883

Printed in Europe, USA, Canada, Australia, Japan

Cover: Foto ©ninafisch / pixelio.de

More available books at **www.hansebooks.com**

THE

SCOTTISH HOUSE OF ROGER

WITH NOTES RESPECTING

THE FAMILIES OF PLAYFAIR AND HALDANE
OF BERMONY

BY THE

REV. CHARLES ROGERS, LL.D.,

HISTORIOGRAPHER TO THE ROYAL HISTORICAL SOCIETY, FELLOW OF THE
SOCIETY OF ANTIQUARIES OF SCOTLAND, AND CORRESPONDING
MEMBER OF THE HISTORICAL AND GENEALOGICAL
SOCIETY OF NEW ENGLAND

SECOND EDITION

EDINBURGH
PRINTED FOR PRIVATE CIRCULATION
1875

THE

SCOTTISH HOUSE OF ROGER,

ETC.

SEVERAL centuries before the introduction of surnames, and
its adoption as a family designation, the name of Roger
was common over Europe. Derived from the Latin words
rudis a rod, and *gero* I bear, the mediæval designation was
Rudiger, signifying seneschal or chamberlain. About the
ninth century the name was abbreviated Roger; a form in
which both as a name and surname it has been used in all
European countries.*

Rolf, Rollo, or Rou, a Danish sea-king, founded the Norman
dynasty at Rouen, to which place he gave name, and where
he reigned sixteen years (A.D. 927 to 943). He was progenitor
of William the Conqueror, and of that illustrious race who
have since the Conquest borne the English sceptre. During
the century following the reign of Rolf at Rouen we find Roger
de Toesny, who claimed descent from Malahulc, uncle of Rolf,
fighting valiantly against the infidels in Spain, and achieving
great victories, not without cruelty and violence. Roger
married the daughter of the widowed Countess of Barcelona,
"a princess," remarks Mr Freeman, " whose dominions were
practically Spanish, though her formal allegiance was due to
the Parisian king. This marriage," Mr Freeman adds, " was

---

* Out of the List compiled by M. Leopold Delisle of the Companions of
William the Conqueror (*Herald and Genealogist*, vol. for 1863), no fewer than
twenty-seven bear the name of " Roger."

doubtless designed as the beginning of a Norman principality in Spain, but the scheme failed to take any lasting root."* On his return from Spain, Roger de Toesny rebelled against William, the future Conqueror, and sent his son, Roger de Bellomont or Beaumont against him. A battle ensued, in which Roger de Toesny and his two sons were slain.†

The latter portion of Mr Freeman's narrative differs from other accounts of the Beaumont family. According to some Norman writers, Roger à la Barbe gave name to the little town of Beaumont le Roger, beautifully situated on the Rille in Normandy. Above this town rises a limestone hill, richly wooded, at the base of which is a fountain named *La Fontaine Roger*. The latter is mentioned in the *dotalitium*, or deed of dower of Countess Judith, wife of Richard, second Duke of Normandy, who bestowed the domain on the Abbey of Bernay, from which it passed into the possession of Humphrey, Seigneur of Vieilles ; which was the head place of the fief till 1040. Roger à la Barbe‡ was the son of Humphrey; he built a castle on the summit of the rocky eminence, and his Christian name thereafter became the family designation of his House. Beaumont le Roger was besieged and captured by Henry I., afterwards by Richard Cœur de Lion ; it was stormed and burned by Philip Augustus, and more than once was made an appanage of the Royal Family of France. Given to Charles the bad, King of Navarre, it was captured by Bertrand du Guesclin, and demolished. Pillaged by Henry V. in 1417, it was in 1651 ceded to the Duke of Bouillon in exchange for the principality of Sedan.§ Roger à la Barbe was one of the Conqueror's chief nobles, and his best counsellor and friend. When William left Normandy to conquer Eng-

* Freeman's Norman Conquest, vol. i., pp. 460, 461.
† *Ibid*, vol. ii., p. 197. See also sheet pedigree prefixed to the Lives of the Lindsays for some information regarding the De Toesnys.
‡ In his Nobiliaire de Normandie, 1666, folio, M. Jacques Louis Chevillard has presented the armorial escutcheon of Roger du Mont Boumonville. The shield is *argent*, on a fesse *sable* three roses of the field ; in base three lions rampant of second two and one ; all within a bordure *gules*.
§ Normandy, its History and Antiquities. Lond.

land, he associated Roger with Matilda, his queen, in the government of his kingdom. Roger helped to plan the expedition, and furnished no fewer than sixty ships for transporting the Norman army. He married in 1045 the heiress of the Count of Mulan, through whom he obtained high power in France as well as in his own kingdom. Robert de Bellomont was one of the sons of Roger à la Barbe ; he is described as grandson of Turolf of Pont Andemare, by Wevia, sister of Gunnora, wife of Richard, first of that name, Duke of Normandy, great-grandfather to William I. He accompanied the Conqueror into England, and mainly contributed to the triumph at Hastings. Robert inherited the earldom of Mellent in Normandy from his mother Adelina, daughter of Waleran, and sister of Hugh, who took the habit of a monk in the Abbey of Bec, both Earls of Mellent. Of the conduct of Robert de Bellomont at Hastings, William Pictaviensis writes : " A certain Norman young soldier, son of Roger de Bellomont, nephew and heir to Hugh, Earl of Mellent, by Adelina his sister, making the first onset in that fight, did what deserveth lasting fame, boldly charging and breaking in upon the enemy with that regiment which he commanded in the right wing of the army," for which gallant services he obtained sixty-four lordships in Warwickshire, sixteen in Leicestershire, and one in Gloucestershire, in all ninety-one. He did not, however, attain the dignity of the English peerage before the reign of Henry I., when that monarch created him Earl of Leicester.*

Besides Robert de Bellomont, founder of the noble House of Leicester, another member of the Beaumont family took part in the Norman Conquest of England. His name of Rougere, or Fitz Roger, is entered on the roll of Battel Abbey.†
Of this person, or his son, we have obtained some particulars in the *Chartulaire de la Basse-Normandie*, and also in a collection of documents relating to Normandy, transcribed from the Norman archives, and deposited in the Public Record Office. To a Latin instrument dated 1076, setting forth the

* Dugdale's Baronage, vol. i., p. 83.   † Lower's English Surnames.

independence of the church of St Leonard against the pretensions of the Bishop of Sieux, Count Roger and Roger de Bellomont appended their names, along with William the Conqueror, Matilda, his queen, and other notable persons. Of this instrument we give the following translation:

"Because the memory of men, like the men themselves, quickly passes away, there are some things which ought to be committed to writing. We, therefore, taking provident care for the future interests of this church, have thought it right to record in this document an event which we are desirous that our successors should be made acquainted with. It happened then, on a certain festival of St Leonard, that Count (Earl) Roger was present, with some eminent persons of both orders, whom he had invited out of respect to himself and to do honour to this church. At the joint request of ourselves and the Count, the Bishop of Sieux sang mass, and coveting the offerings, tried to appropriate them. Observing which, and horrified at it as something monstrous, we forcibly, and with reproaches, seized them from the person—one of his clergy—to whose keeping he had intrusted them. Enraged at this, he declared he would excommunicate both us and our church. He fulfilled his threat, and before Count Roger could complain of the bishop's proceedings to the Archbishop of Rouen, we, in order to smooth matters, betook ourselves on a set day to Rouen, and there, in the palace and in the presence of the King and Queen of England, Count Robert charged the Bishop of Sieux of having without just cause presumed to excommunicate the church of St Leonard. The bishop retorted that we were to blame, as he had a clear and legal right to all the offerings collected in his diocese, and that we had done him a wrong by taking from him ours. On this the king and queen conferred with Count Roger on the state of his church, when he, together with those present, clearly narrated how that William de Bellasis had built the aforesaid church for the remission of his sins, and how that by an order of Pope Leo, of blessed memory, it had been constituted free and independent, and that from the day of its dedication neither archbishop nor bishop had any customary right in it, nor in any way over it, the power of excommunication. They asserted, moreover, that very old men who had seen and heard all this were ready to corroborate these statements to the satisfaction of the king's judgment.　Hearing this, the king and queen gave orders that John, the archbishop, Roger de Bellomont, and many other barons, should give sentence according to the evidence.　And they, counsel taken, judge that a church of such high authority, and with rights conferred by so many illustrious ancestors, had been free, and that having enjoyed its liberty for so long a time, it ought to enjoy it in perpetuity; that the bishop had not only done an injury to Count Roger, but also to the king, of whom he held the church.　John, the archbishop, further said that there were some churches in his own diocese in which he had no rights at all.　Accordingly Robert, Bishop of Sieux, had to atone for the crime with which he was chargeable against the king and Count Roger in invading the privileges of the aforesaid church. It was also there decreed that if either archbishop or bishop should hereafter presume to disturb it, he should by apostolical and royal authority be separated from the communion of the faithful till such time as he had made satisfaction.　This have approved William, King, and Matilda, Queen; John, Archbishop of Rouen; Robert, Bishop of Sieux; Count Roger; Robert de Bellasis; Roger de Bellomont; Curvisus, William, and Hascuin, canons; with Arnelland, and many others."*

Roger, son of Thorold, or Torold, is celebrated in a document, preserved in the archives of Normandy,† of which we present a translation :

"Donation to the (house of the) Holy Trinity of Rouen, by permission of William, King of England.

"Roger, son of Torold, about to travel with Count William to parts beyond the mountains, gave for the health of his soul three acres of land in Southvill to the monks of the Holy Trinity of Rouen, reserving no feudal rights, but dying on the passage, and being thereby prevented from confirming his grant, it was graciously confirmed in his stead by one William Trenchefoil, knight in his train, William, King of the English, assenting. ✠ The seal of King William, ✠ the seal of William Trenchefoil, ✠ the seal of Bernard the Forester.

" Witnesses, Richard Osbern and Roger the bishop ✠."

* Chartulaire de la Basse-Normandie, vol. i. p. 49, vol. i. p. 80. (Plaids royaux ver l'année 1076. Archives d'Alençon.)

† See Transcripts of Charters and other Documents, from various Archives of Normandy, in the Public Record Office, London.

Immediately after the Norman Conquest persons of the House of Roger de Beaumont spread rapidly over England. Roger, Archdeacon of Shrewsbury (Rogerus, Archid. de Salopesber), is between the years 1162 and 1182 witness to a legal instrument.* From this early period persons bearing the name of Roger were extensively connected with the Church. Roger, styled *de Pont l'Evêque* in Normandy,† was Archbishop of York, 1154-1181. An ambitious churchman, his career is intimately bound up with the civil and ecclesiastical history of the kingdom. A native of Kent, he first appears under public notice in the family or court of Theobald, Archbishop of Canterbury. Here he had among his companions a young priest, who was subsequently to become his rival—the celebrated Thomas à Becket.‡ When Henry II. determined that his eldest son Henry should be crowned during his lifetime, he requested Archbishop Roger to perform the ceremony, owing to his quarrel with Becket, who, as primate, was entitled to the honour. Becket hastened to anathematize Roger and two of the chief prelates who assisted him, an event which led to Becket's assassination by those who sought to vindicate the rights of the northern province.§ It is proper to add, that Roger of York proved that he was not accessory to the murder of his rival. He possessed no small share of military ardour. In 1174 he took a prominent part in the wars of the north ; he welcomed the barons who proceeded against William the Lion, and to Henry II. sent intelligence of his capture.‖ For his military zeal, Henry, in 1177, bestowed on him the castles of Scarborough and Roxburgh.¶ Bishop Roger of St Andrews, 1188-1202, was second son of Robert, third Earl of Leicester, and cousin to King William of Scotland, who made him first his Chancellor, then

---

* Collectanea Genealogica, vol. iv. p. 15.

† Fasti Eboracenses, by the Rev. W. H. Dixon, edited by the Rev. James Raine. London, 1863. 8vo, vol. i., p. 233.

‡ Fasti Eboracenses, vol. i., p. 233.

§ Dean Stanley's Historical Memorials of Westminster Abbey, pp. 52, 53.

‖ Chronique de Jordan Fantosme, ed. Surtees Society, pp. 78, 79, 91, 93.

¶ Hoveden, 323*b* ; Benedict Patrib., 203.

Abbot of Melrose, and afterwards Bishop of St Andrews. He founded the Castle of St Andrews as a residence for himself and his successors.* From 1199 till 1201 he resided chiefly in England, his name often occurring during these years as a witness to charters granted by King John to various public bodies.†

The Norman name of Roger travelled northward. Prior to his accession to the Scottish throne in 1124, David, Earl of Huntingdon, resided in England. There he married Matilda, heiress of Walthcof, Earl of Northumberland, procuring through this alliance estates in Northumberland, Cumberland, and Huntingdon. On his accession he introduced to important offices in his kingdom persons of English or Norman extraction, with whom he had associated during his sojourn in the south. Among these was Hugh de Morville, whom he constituted Constable of Scotland. He was son of Roger de Morville and grandson of Simon de Morville, who possessed the barony of Burgh-on-the-Sands, in Cumberland. Richard, a younger brother of Simon de Morville, took part with the King of Scotland and Robert, Earl of Leicester, in the hostilities carried on against Henry II. by the young king.‡

In addition to the high office of constable, with power to lead the king's army, Hugh de Morville received extensive estates in Tweeddale, Lauderdale, and the Lothians, in the south-east, and in Clydesdale and Ayrshire in the south-west, of Scotland. He married Beatrix Beauchamp (de Campo Bello), daughter of a powerful family of Norman settlers in Scotland, and the reputed founders of the ducal House of Argyle. By this marriage was born a son, Richard de Morville, who became principal Minister of State to William the Lion.§

Hugh de Morville resembled his royal patron, David I., in

* Wyntoun's Chronicle, *passim.*
† Rotuli Chartarum in turri Londinensi.
‡ Dugdale.
§ Chalmers's Caledonia, vol. i., pp. 503, 504.

religious devotedness. He founded the Abbey of Kilwinning,
in Ayrshire, and the Abbey of Dryburgh, in the county of
Roxburgh. At the period of the latter foundation (1150) we
are first introduced to the name of Roger on Scottish soil. In
the Register of Dryburgh (Liber S. Marie de Dryburgh) occur
numerous entries in reference to the acquisition of lands by
Richard de Morville from Roger, "Janitor de Rogesburgh"
(Roxburgh). In the royal charter of foundation, David I.
granted and confirmed to the aforesaid brothers that portion of land which Beatrix de Beauchamp bought of Roger
the Janitor, and gave to them as a free and perpetual
benefaction.

The janitor of a religious house was distributor of the alms
of the institution, for the poor were supplied *ad portam monas-
terii ;* [*] he also kept the keys, and had power to refuse
admission to those whom he deemed unworthy. Roger,
"Janitor de Rogesburgh," was a landowner of considerable
extent; and therefore, independently of his ecclesiastical
position, a person of consequence. His name implies his
English descent, while his transactions with Beatrix de Beauchamp, mother of Richard de Morville, before the construction
of Dryburgh Abbey, would imply that he was a person of
considerable age at the period of the Abbey's foundation. He
bore the same name as the father of Hugh de Morville; and
the first Abbot of Dryburgh, who was nominated by Hugh,
was a churchman named Roger. The coincidence is sufficiently
singular; but it would be rash on account of it to assume that
Roger the Janitor was a relative of the De Morvilles, or that
the Janitor of Roxburgh Church was subsequently Abbot of
Dryburgh Abbey.

Abbot Roger of Dryburgh took office on the 13th December
1152.[†] During his incumbency he received three bulls from
Pope Alexander III., confirming grants to the abbey, and
there permitting service during a general interdict. He resigned his office as abbot in 1177 ; and proceeded to England,

---

* Scotch Legal Antiquities, by Cosmo Innes, 1872, 8vo, p. 170.
† Liber S. Marie de Dryburgh.

probably under the patronage of Archbishop Roger of York, who was, like himself, a favourite of Alexander III., the reigning Pope.

In 1236 "Dominus Rogerus Cellerarius" was translated from Melrose to the Abbey of Neubothel (Newbottle).* Abbot Roger of Newbottle assisted at the conference which took place at Roxburgh between Henry III. of England and Alexander III. of Scotland, on the 20th September 1255. He attended a chapter of his order held in England, and on his return towards Scotland, died at the Monastery of Vandy in 1256.† "Rogerus, Abbas de Dryburgh" is witness to a charter along with William de Lamberton, Bishop of St Andrews, whose episcopate extended from 1298 to 1328.‡

Before proceeding further, it is essential that we make some observations respecting the origin of surnames. According to Du Chesne, the lords of France began to assume the names of their demesnes so early as the year 989. Camden relates that surnames were first used in England under Edward the Confessor. A great impulse to the use of surnames was given by the Norman adventurers, many of whom assumed as family designations the names of *Chateaux*, or Villages, on the other side of the Channel. At the Domesday Valuation surnames were not uncommon ; they were frequent among persons of rank in England in the middle of the twelfth century.§ In Scotland they were not common till half a century later. Ordinary persons took names from their occupations, or their localities ; ‖ but those who possessed Norman blood preferred as surnames the designations of their ancestral homes, or their own Christian names.

Early in the fourteenth century flourished in or near the

* Registrum S. Marie de Neubotle, 1140-1528. Edin. 1849, 4to, p. 154.
† Chronica de Mailros.
‡ Chalmers's Caledonia, *passim.*
§ An Essay on Family Nomenclature by Mark Antony Lower. Lond., 1849, 12mo, vol. i., p. 31.
‖ Inquisitiones Nonarum, 1340 (13th Edward III.).

town of Roxburgh a landowner known as "Roger of Auldton." Surnames were now in universal use, and Roger had doubtless been for some time the family designation of the owner of the *auld toon*, or old town, of Roxburgh. The "old town" of Melrose in Roxburghshire still exists. An ancestor of Roger of Auldton had doubtless built the original place or village of Roxburgh—hence the designation of his descendant. It is, indeed, not improbable that the original settler—probably Roger the Janitor—gave name to the entire province. The old name of Roxburgh was Marken.* In charters of the reign of David I. it is designated "Rogysburgh"—which is precisely the pronunciation that would now be given by Scottish Borderers to the word Rogersburgh.† We offer the conjecture to solve an etymological difficulty.‡

In 1328, Robert de Colvil, "Lord of Oxenham, quitclaimed to Roger of Auldton, near Roxburgh, an annual revenue of five shillings in which he was bound for two oxgangs of land, which he held of him in the town and territory of Heton, granting also to the said Roger the liberty of converting the two oxgangs to pious uses."§ During the same year Roger of Auldton obtained a "quitclaim" from John de Valays,

* Holinshead's Scottish Chronicle, 1805, vol. i., p. 1367.

† Origines Parochiales, vol. i., *passim*.

‡ There has been considerable discussion as to the origin of the name Roxburgh. Some maintain that it is a corruption of Rose-burgh, a place of primroses ; others, that Roch, a saint, had his cell in the locality ; others, that being the head-quarters of Border thieves, it was at first styled Rogues-burgh. In confirmation of our own theory, it may be remarked that the name of Roger was common among the old landowners of the south-eastern Border. In a Jury summoned by Alexander III. in 1262 for determining a dispute between the burgesses of Peebles and the laird of Crockston relative to the digging of peat, occur the names of Roger of Kedistun, and Roger the gardener. In the Ragman Rolls (1291-1296) are inserted, in connection with the south-eastern district, the names of Roger le Mareschal, and Rogier de Mohaut (W. Chambers's History of Peeblesshire. Edin., 8vo., 1864, pp. 50, 64). A place near Lauder, which belonged to Dry-burgh Abbey, was known as Roger's Law (Liber S. Marie de Dryburgh, p. 325). There is a Roger's Crag near Halmyre, in Peeblesshire, (Chambers's "Peebles-shire," p. 43).

§ Liber de Calchou ; Register of Kelso, pp. 369, 370. *Origines Parochiales Scotia*, vol. i., *passim*.

whereby he was freed from an annual payment of "two pence yearly for two oxgangs of land" which Roger's father, Gilbert, had undertaken to pay to Henry, father of John.* With lands at Auldton of Roxburgh Roger proceeded in 1329 to endow "a chantry of one priest, who should ever after perform Divine service in Saint James's church, Roxburgh."† For endowment he granted "all his lands, revenues and posses-sions in the town and territory of Auldton, together with the whole demesnes which he held in the said territory." This grant was confirmed by charters from King Robert the Bruce and the Bishop of Glasgow ; and Margaret, wife of the donor, to indicate her approval, made an addition to the grant and stipulated that, "forty pounds of silver should be paid to the fabric of the cathedral church of Glasgow" if she or her heirs should revoke it. The entire annual endowments provided for the chantry by Roger of Auldton and his wife amounted to £20 Scots, or about £200 of present money.‡

Long as they had been settled in Scotland, the members of the House of Roger remembered whence they had sprung. In 1360 the church of Old Roxburgh was granted by Edward I. to Roger of Bromley.§ From the vicinity of Bromley (county of Kent) came Archbishop Roger of York, the close ally of Roger de Morville, whose son Hugh is said to have avenged his quarrel with Thomas à Becket. At Bromley the House of Roger was planted in the time of the Conqueror, and there members of the family continued to live prosperously for cen-turies. At least one family of the name is still resident in the locality.‖ In a sasine of the burgh of Berwick dated 1291-92, Roger is named as Keeper (Custos) under Edward I.¶ In

* Origines Parochiales, vol. i., pp. 452-460.

† Liber de Calchou, p. 368; Regist. Glasg., p. 244.

‡ Origines Parochiales, vol. i., pp. 452-460.

§ Rotuli Scotiæ, vol. i., p. 852. Origines Parochiales, vol. i., p. 453.

‖ To Colonel Joseph L. Chester, author of the "Life of John Rogers, the first Martyr of the English Reformation," we are indebted for copious extracts from the parish register of Bromley in connection with the Roger family from 1582 to 1666.

¶ Chronica de Mailros.

the counties of Roxburgh, Berwick, and Selkirk, persons of
the name are occasionally to be found. But the main branch
of the House migrated westward. The period and circum-
stances of that migration we shall show presently.

In his "History of Ayrshire and its Families," Mr James
Paterson writes,* "During the reign of Robert the Bruce, and
before 1321, Eustacia de Colvil, relict of Sir Reginald le
Chene, and daughter and heiress of Sir William Colvil of
Ochiltree,† granted to the monks of Melrose the church and
church lands of Ochiltree ; and the grant was confirmed by a
charter of Robert de Colvil of Oxnam and Ochiltree. This
Robert de Colvil of Oxnam is the same who, as 'Lord of
Oxenham,' quitclaimed in 1328 to Roger of Auldton an
annual revenue of five shillings for lands in the town and
territory of Heton." He held lands both in the counties of
Roxburgh and Ayr, having succeeded to the territory of the
Morvilles in those counties. At the period when he granted
lands at Ochiltree to Melrose Abbey, the head of that estab-
lishment was Abbot Roger,‡ a member, no doubt, of the
church-loving family of Auldton. Probably through his
recommendation Robert de Colvil, as a good son of the
Church, made the quitclaim to Roger of Auldton of his feu-
rent of the lands at Heton; and it is not unreasonable to con-
clude that the same generous churchman planted some of his
kindred on the newly-acquired church lands at Ochiltree,
where they were found long afterwards. It was a practice of
churchmen to oblige their relations by providing them with
easy holdings on the church lands. To the abbey of Dryburgh, and Roger, its first abbot, David I. granted a manor at

---

* Paterson's History of Ayrshire, vol. ii., p. 394.

† Liber de Melrose, p. 343.

‡ Lord Blachford of Wisdome, formerly Sir Frederick Rogers, Bart., a representative of the Roger family in England, is married to a daughter of Mr Colvile
of Ochiltree, whose progenitor granted to the monks of Melrose his lands of
Ochiltree, thereby affording a home and headquarters to a family, a member of
which has, after five centuries, become allied in marriage to an ennobled descendant
of the sept.

Carail (Crail),* Fifeshire, and there the patronymic of Roger still remains.†

The church lands of Ochiltree were retained by the monks of Melrose till the period of the Reformation,‡ and so long did members of the Roger family find headquarters in that Ayrshire parish. In the first volume of the Commissariat Register of Glasgow is recorded the will of Alexander Roger in Ochiltree, made in 1549 or 1550. From the inventory of his goods he appears to have been a substantial farmer. The inventory includes "one horse, three mares, four oxen, eight cows, two stirks (young bullocks), nineteen sheep, forty bolls of oats, five and a half bolls of barley, and household goods to the value of fifty pounds." In his will he bequeaths *fourpence* "to the building of St Kentigern." Between 1153 and 1160 Malcolm IV. granted "to the church of St Kentigern, Glasgow, and to Bishop Herbert and his successors, the church of Old Rokesburgh, with all its appurtenances."§ And in virtue of this connection between the church of Old Roxburgh and the cathedral of St Kentigern at Glasgow, we find Margaret, wife of Roger of Auldton, stipulating, in 1329, that the sum of forty pounds of silver should be paid to the fabric of the cathedral if she or her heirs should revoke her supplementary grant to the chantry of St James's Church, Roxburgh.‖ So in after generations did Alexander Roger, as a faithful son of the Church, and a descendant of the pious laird of Auldton, feel called on to remember the fabric of St Kentigern.¶

A member of the House of Roger was a distinguished pioneer of the Scottish Reformation, and one of its martyrs. He is thus described by John Knox: "Johne Roger, a Blake Freir, godly, learned, and ane that had fructfully preached

* Liber S. Marie de Dryburgh.

† Baptismal Registers of Crail, and of the adjacent parishes of Kingsbarns and Anstruther.

‡ Paterson's Ayrshire, vol. ii., p. 394.

§ Regist. Glasg., p. 14.   See *ante.*

¶ In his Testament, 12th July 1547, Allan Stewart, in Allanton, bequeaths "4 pennies to the fabric of S. Kentigern." Among his creditors is "Alexander Roger," to the amount of 6s.

Christ Jesus to the comforte of many in Anguss and Mearnes, whom that bloody man (Cardinal Beaton) caused murther in the ground of the Sea-toure of Sanctandross, and then caused to cast him ower the craig, sparsing a fals bruyt (report) that the said Johne seeking to flie had broken his awin craig."[*] John Roger suffered in 1544, eleven years prior to the martyr-dom of his namesake and remote relative, John Rogers, the English proto-martyr, who was burned at Smithfield on the 4th February 1555. He was in all probability a member of the Blackfriars Monastery at Dundee, whence the report of his preaching would readily reach Cardinal Beaton at St Andrews, a town distant from Dundee eleven Scottish miles.

Andrew Stewart, third Lord Ochiltree, usually styled "the good Lord," was a zealous promoter of the Reformation. His daughter, Margaret Stewart, became second wife of John Knox; the marriage took place in March 1564, when the Reformer was in his fifty-eighth year. "The good Lord" may have been enlightened in the Reformed doctrines by the con-verted Black Friar, who was doubtless a scion of the family of Roger at Ochiltree.

Lord Ochiltree's estates were situated in the parish and district of Ochiltree, Ayrshire. Between 1570 and 1592 he received four charters of lands and baronies at Ochiltree, in-cluding the church lands of the parish.[†] These facts enable us to trace the migration of the Roger family, for in the will of David Roger "in Redie,"[‡] Forfarshire, dated 24th May 1581, the testator enumerates among his creditors "my Lord Ochiltree for 4 bollis, 2 firlottis, teind beir." He had paid this amount in feu-duty for lands situated on Lord Ochiltree's estate at Ochiltree. The reference serves to show that the testator had hailed from Ochiltree, and had then occupied some position as a landholder. In his will, David Roger mentions Lord Seltoun as "maister of the grund," that is, landlord of his farm occupied by him at Airlie.

The family of Roger at Redie were, we shall find, allied to

* John Knox's Works, edited by David Laing, LL.D., vol. i., p. 119.
† Paterson's Ayrshire Families.   ‡ Com. Reg. of Edinburgh.

a family of the name, occupying lands which belonged to the Cistercian Abbey of Coupar-Angus. In 1526 Donald Campbell, fourth son of Archibald, second Earl of Argyle, was appointed abbot of Coupar. From his connection with the west of Scotland, it is believed that he invited a member of the Roger family at Ochiltree to undertake the office of *conversus* or steward of his religious house. Like "the good Lord Ochiltree," he was favourable to the Reformed doctrines, and on this account he may have more readily extended his patronage to a family which had produced a friar willing to endure persecution or death in attestation of his faith.

At the time of his death in 1562, William Roger was tenant-farmer at Coupar-Grange, as is attested in his will afterwards to be quoted. That he occupied the grange or home farm of the abbey, denotes the nature of his office prior to the secularisation of the lands. The grange farm was held by the steward in right of his office. He superintended not only the *nativi* or serfs but acted as chamberlain of the institution, receiving rents from the tenants and conducting the entire business of the estates. In the lay brotherhood he held a foremost rank.

Donald Campbell, Abbot of Coupar, attended the Parliament of August 1560, which annulled the Roman Church.* From the possessions of the abbey he granted lands to each of his five illegitimate sons,† while on the grange farm he retained at the former rent of £22, 11s. 10d. Scots, William Roger, the abbey steward.

William Roger died at Coupar-Grange in 1562. At the time of his decease, his personal estate was valued at £452, 18s. 6d. Scots, exclusive of "silver lent to the laird of Ruthven," probably his wife's dowry. His will, with the corresponding inventory, is a document of sufficient interest to be presented entire. It is as follows :‡

"The Testament testamentar and Inventar of the guidis geir soumis of money and debtis pertaining to umquhil William Roger, in

---

* Acta Parl., vol. ii., p. 599.   † Jervise's Angus and Mearns, p. 396.
‡ Edinburgh Commissariat Register.

B

Couper Grange in Angus the tyme of his decease, quha deceasit in the month of Junij the year of God 1562 years faithfully maid and given up by himself as containing the nomination of executors and inventory of his guidis and pairtlie maid and given up by Marjorie Blair his relict and William Roger his sone as containing the debtis awand to him and be him quhome he nominat his Executors in his latter Will underwritten, of the daitt at Couper Grange the 16th day of Apryll the year of God foresaid before thir witnesses Alexander Cumming, George Ewan, William Quhittsoun, John Quhittsoun his neibouris with utheris diverse.

" In the first the said umquhil William Roger had the guidis geir soumis of money and debtis of the avail and prices after following perteyning to him at the tyme of his decease foresaid, viz. 8 oxin, price of the peece 6 lib summa 48 lib. Item 3 ky, price of the peece 4 lib summa 12 lib. Item ane horse, twa meres ane foall by the heirezeld horse,* price of them 16 lib. Item 9 stottis and queyis, twa and three years auld, price of the peece oure heide 4 merkis, summa 24 lib; 6 auld scheip price of the peece 13s. 4d. summa 4 lib; Item 24 hoggis price of the peece 6s. 8d. summa 8 lib. Item sawin on the ground 40 bollis aittis, estimat to the third corne extending to 6 score bollis aittis, price of the boll with the fodder 20s., summa 120 lib. Item mair 15 bollis beir sawin estimat to the fird (fourth) corne extending to sixty bollis beir price of the bolle with the fodder 30s. summa 90 lib; Item in peis 58 lib mony. Item in utensils and domicilis with the abulzements of his bodye estimat to three score pundis. Summa of the Inventar 440 lib.

" Followis the debtis awand to the deid. Item, there wes awand to the said umquhil William Roger be William Quhittsoun in Couper Grange 20 merkis—Item Mair be him 6 libs for whilk he is actit in the officials bookis of Dunkeld.

" Item be John Guthrie 42s.

" Summa of the debtis awand to the deid 20 lib 3 : 6d.

" Summa of the Inventar with the debtis 460 lib 3 : 8d.

" Followis the debtis awand be the deid.

" Item, ther wes awand be the said umquhil William Roger to the Abbey of Couper for the ferm of the grund in anno 1562 15 bollis 1 peck beir at 30s. the boll, summa 22 libs 11s. 10d.

" Mair 3 bollis aittis at 20s. the boll, summa 3 libs. Item Mair

---

* A horse which the lord of the manor had a right to claim.

for the teind in anno foresaid 12 bollis victuall thereof 5 bollis beir and 7 bollis meal at 30s. the bolle over heid—summa 18 libs.

"Item, to his servants for the rest of their yearis fee and bountith, viz. to Johne Simpson, 30s. to Robert Spence 30s. and to Margaret Moncur 13s. 4d.

"Summa of the debtis awand to the deid 27 lib. 5s. 2d. Restis of free geir the debtis deductit 432 lib. 18s. 6d. to be dividit in three partis ; the deid's part* is 144 libs 6s. 1d. whereof the quot is componed for four libs.

"Follow the Deids legacy and latter will.

"At Couper Grange the 16th day of April the yeir of God 1562 yeirs the whilk day the said William Roger made his legacy and latter will as follows :

"I leave Executors and Intromitters my wife Marjorie Blair and my son William Roger. I mak Oversmen David Roger in Redie William Roger his son Johne Diksoune and Johne Broun to see that the Executors do that they aucht to do to the bairnis and the gudewyf als lang as she halds hir but ane man to be maister of the hale hous. The silver that is in the Laird of Ruthven's hands gif it happens to be delyverit in the gudewyf's tyme, the gudeman and the gudewyf are content that it be delyverit to the bairnis and disponit to them quha hes mister† be sight of the Oversmen. And this baith the gudeman and the gudewyf is content hereof with the advice of all the Oversmen together.

"This was done before thir witnesses Alexander Cumming, George Ewen, William Quhittsoun, John Quhittsoun, his neibouris with utheris divers. Sic subscribitur, William Roger. The above Will was confirmed before the Commissary at Dunkeld on the 18th July 1583."

David Roger "in Redie," one of the oversmen in William Roger's will, has already been referred to. He tenanted the considerable farm of Redie in Airlie, a parish belonging to the

---

* The "deid's part" is that portion of a man's movable estate which he is entitled to dispose of by testament. If a man leaves a widow and no children, the widow is entitled to one-half of the free movables as her *jus relictæ*. If children are left and no widow, one-half of the free movables go to the child or children as *legitim*. When both widow and children are left, the widow has a third as a *jus relictæ*, the child a third as *legitim*, and the remaining third constitutes "the dead's part," which may be disposed of by will according to inclination.

† Need.

Ogilvies, and from which the chief of that House—the Earl of Airlie—derives his title. On the 23d September 1540 the abbot, Donald Campbell, confirmed James, Lord Ogilvy of Airlie, in the office of hereditary bailie of the regality of the abbey of Coupar.* Through the good offices of Lord Ogilvy, David Roger was, as a relative of the abbey steward, settled as a farmer in Airlie parish. David Roger died on the 26th February 1582. By his will he constituted his elder son William his sole executor, and, excepting 200 merks to his younger son David, endowed him with his "haill guidis." William Roger died in February 1589, his free substance at the time of his decease amounting to £1456 Scots. To his son John he bequeathed the lease of his farm, but his son James appears to have obtained the principal portion of his estate. In 1606 the latter executed a settlement of his affairs, in which he specifies that should his sons die before succeeding him in his "rowme" or inheritance, his daughters should be permitted to enjoy the succession, only on the condition that should they marry, their husbands should bear the name of Roger.† James Roger determined to establish a family, but did not succeed. Members of his House remained at Airlie till the beginning of the present century, when they became extinct in the male line.‡

At the Reformation the lands of the abbey of Coupar were divided into twelve portions.§ The grange farm, one of the twelve—which had constituted the farm of William Roger—became the property of his son William, who, by William Roger of Redie, in his will executed in 1589, is styled "portioner of Coupar-Grange." The estate was doubtless purchased with the money for which his parents held a bond from the Laird of Ruthven.

By the extinction of the House of Roger of Redie, elder branch of the Rogers of Ochiltree, the representation of the family reverted to the Rogers of Coupar-Grange. William

---

* Jervise's Angus and Mearns, p. 397.   † Edinburgh Com. Reg., 1610.
‡ Marriage and Baptismal Register of Airlie.
§ New Statistical Account of Scotland, vol. x., p. 1190.

Roger, portioner of Coupar-Grange, is in 1589* styled by
William Roger of Redie his "brother-in-law;" which would
imply that even a few years after the Reformation the marriage
of cousins was not distasteful. William Roger of Coupar-
Grange was father of two sons, William, his successor, and
George. The latter proceeded to Dundee, and there engaged
in merchandise and shipping. He died in 1611, aged thirty-
three; his tombstone in the old burial-ground of Dundee is
inscribed thus: "Hic · dormienti · pietate · et · virtvte · insigni ·
viro · Georgio · Roger · Navclero · et · civi · hvivs · oppidi · qvi · obiit ·
anno · 1611 · die · primo · Octobris · ætatis · vero · svæ · anno · 33 ·
hoc · faciendvm · procvravit · eivs · conivnx · Elizabetha · Loch-
malovnie · Mihi · hodie · cras · tibi." By his wife, Elizabeth Loch-
malonie, he left one son, William, who became a prosperous
merchant at Dundee, and held office in the magistracy. He
married Euphan, daughter of James Mann, merchant, maternal
aunt of William Duncan, of Seaside, progenitor of the Earls of
Camperdown. *Bailie* William Roger mortified or bequeathed
in 1658 "one half of his real and personal estate" for the educa-
tion and training of seven "poor male children" within the
burgh. The fund is at present £1745, 7s. 3d. Bailie Roger's
widow established, in 1663, a Merchants' Widows Fund at
Dundee, of which the present stock is £2452, 4s. 10d.†
William Roger, second "portioner" of Coupar-Grange, married
Elspeth Angus, by whom he became father of George Roger,
who was baptized on the 28th January 1649.‡ William
Roger died of "the Plague," a pestilent sickness which visiting
the country in 1664 decimated the population. His widow
disposed of the family estate to a prosperous tradesman.
George Roger continued to reside on the estate till his death
in 1710. He married Catherine Bisset, and had issue four sons,
William, Charles, James, and Patrick, and three daughters,
Anne, Margaret, and Janet. Anne, the eldest daughter, born
May 1680, married John Davie, parish of Coupar-Angus, and

* Will of William Roger of Redie, formerly quoted.
† Report on Charitable Institutions at Dundee, pp. 9, 10.
‡ Baptismal Register of Bendochy.

had issue. The second daughter, Margaret, born April 1682, married John Stewart, farmer, Greendykes, Perthshire, with issue. Janet, the youngest daughter, baptized 19th September 1686, married, 1st April 1709, James Playfair, farmer, Couttie in the parish of Bendochy, Perthshire, by whom she became mother of six sons, George, James, Patrick, William, Charles, and John, and five daughters, Catherine, Barbara, Margaret, Isobel, and Janet. Of the sons, James, Patrick, William, and John died unmarried. This matrimonial union between the family of Roger and Playfair was followed by others, so much so that the genealogical history of the two septs became for a series of generations nearly identical.

The name Playfair, anciently Playford, is obviously of Scandinavian origin. William Playfere, of Kent,* married Alice, daughter of William Wood of Bolling, Kent, about the middle of the sixteenth century. Their son, Thomas, was born about the year 1561.† He entered St John's College, Cambridge, in 1584, and after obtaining D.D. and various preferments, was, in 1596, elected Margaret Professor of Divinity. He became chaplain to King James, and was successively rector of Chean, in Surrey, and of Shipdam, in Norfolk. He died on the 2d February 1609, and was buried in St Botolph's Church, Cambridge, where, on a tombstone representing his bust, is a long eulogistic epitaph, partly in Latin verse. He published many separate discourses, which have been repeatedly published in a collected form, and composed a work on Predestination, which was published posthumously. He is thus celebrated by Phineas Fletcher :

" Who lives with death, by Death in death is lying ;
But he who living dies, best lives by dying,
Who life to truth, who death to sorrow gives
In life may die, by death more surely lives.
    My soul in heaven breathes, in schools my fame ;
    Then on my tombe write nothing but my name. "

Playfair's signature is preserved in an old album, belonging to Dr David Laing of Edinburgh, thus—" *Thomas Playfcrus,*

* Fuller's Worthies of England. Lond., 2 vols., 4to, vol. i., p. 509.
† Athenæ Cantabrigiensis, by Charles Henry Cooper, vol. ii., p. 513.

Professor Theologiæ, pro Dᵃ Margareta," with the date, "August 3, 1603."

A supposed relative of the Margaret Professor was the Rev. Andrew Playfair, minister of Aberdalgie,* Perthshire. After studying at the University of St Andrews, where he laureated in 1600, he joined the Scottish Church, but, in token of his Anglican proclivities, he, on obtaining presentation to his charge in 1613, accepted episcopal ordination. He was born about 1580, and died about 1658. He left a son, Andrew, and a daughter, Margaret. Of his son we have no account. The daughter married George Halyburton, of the family of Pitcur, and cousin of George, Bishop of Dunkeld. He succeeded his father as minister of Aberdalgie, but was deprived in 1662 for nonconformity; he died in 1682. Mrs Halyburton was "remarkable for her knowledge, memory of the Scriptures, and gift of prayer." Her son was the eminent and pious Professor Thomas Halyburton of St Andrews, author of "The Great Concern of Salvation."

James Playfair, farmer at Couttie, Perthshire, was connected with the family of the Rev. Andrew Playfair, minister of Aberdalgie, but the precise line of his descent has not been traced. His brother John rented a farm at Coupar-Grange. He married Jean Ure, and was father of four sons, Patrick, Charles, James, and John. James was baptized 25th February 1714, studied at the University of St Andrews, and obtained license as a probationer of the Church 6th September 1739. He was ordained minister of the united parishes of Liff and Benvie 2d March 1743, and died 28th May 1772. By his marriage with Margaret Young he had seven sons, of whom five attained maturity—viz., John, Robert, William, Andrew, and James,—and three daughters, Margaret and Barbara, and a daughter who died young. John, the eldest son, was born 10th March 1748, and was educated at the University of St Andrews. In his eighteenth year he became candidate for the Professorship of Mathematics in Marischal College, Aberdeen, and though unsuccessful, highly

* Scott's Fasti Ecclesiæ Scoticanæ, vol. ii., p. 620.

distinguished himself in a public competition. In 1773 he was ordained minister of Liff and Benvie, in succession to his father. In 1785 he was appointed joint Professor of Mathematics in the University of Edinburgh, a chair which he exchanged for that of Natural Philosophy in 1805. He died unmarried 19th July 1819. He published "Elements of Geometry," "Outlines of Natural Philosophy," and many other valuable scientific works. He is commemorated by a monument on the Calton Hill of Edinburgh.

Robert, second son of the Rev. James Playfair of Liff and Benvie, married Margaret Macniven. Their son, William H. Playfair, was architect of Donaldson's Hospital, the New College, and other public buildings at Edinburgh. He died 18th March 1857. William Playfair, a younger son of the Rev. James Playfair of Liff and Benvie, and brother of Professor Playfair, was an ingenious mechanic, and an eminent miscellaneous writer. He was born in 1759, and died 11th February 1823. He married, and left sons and daughters. John, youngest brother of the Rev. James Playfair, married Catherine, daughter of John Moncur, farmer, Nether-town of Coupar-Grange, by whom he became father of two sons, Patrick and John, and of five daughters, Isabel, Grizel, Elizabeth, Jean, and Catherine.

Charles, fourth son of James Playfair and Janet Roger, was baptized 26th April 1721. He rented the farm of Muirton, parish of Bendochy. He married, 3d July 1750, Catherine Henderson, parish of Blairgowrie, and had issue ten sons, James, George, Charles, David (died in infancy), John (died in infancy), David, John, William, Ebenezer, and Peter; and two daughters, Margaret and Catherine. Margaret, elder daughter, born December 1768, married John Hill of Cotton, in the county of Forfar, and had issue two sons, John and David, and two daughters, Catherine and Anne. John Hill, the elder son, born 1793, succeeded his father in the estate of Cotton; he died, unmarried, in 1847. He was succeeded by his brother David, who was born in 1801, and died, unmarried, in 1860. Catherine, elder daughter, died young; Anne, younger daughter, born in 1798, married James Thomas, solicitor, Perth, and died in 1840, leaving two sons and two daughters. Catherine, younger daughter of Charles Playfair and Catherine Henderson, married John Clarke, farmer, Balbrogie, and had issue. James, eldest son of Charles Playfair, and grandson of Janet Roger, baptized 3d May 1752, was licensed 6th August 1777, and ordained minister of Bendochy 7th February 1791. He composed a work on the culture and management of bees, the MS. of which was unhappily destroyed by fire in the printing-office; he had bestowed twenty years on its preparation, and could not be induced to make an effort towards retrieving his loss. On the 19th December 1790, he married Grizel Duncan, by whom he had four sons, Patrick, Charles, James, and George, and a daughter, Catherine. He died 22d April 1812.

George, eldest son of James Playfair and Janet Roger, rented the farm of Knowhead, or West Bendochy. He married his cousin, Jean Roger (see *postea*).

David, sixth son of Charles Playfair, and grandson of Janet Roger, born March 1765, rented the farm of Hill of Couttie, parish of Bendochy; he married, and had issue. Peter, the youngest son, emigrated to the West Indies, and there died, *s. p.*

Charles, second son of George Roger and Catherine Bisset, born June 1689, married, first, Grizel Mackie, June 1716, and secondly, Margaret Hill, parish of Eassie, March 1718. By his second marriage he had issue two children, John and Catherine, who both died young. James, third son of George Roger, born April 1691, died unmarried, 2d December 1706, and is commemorated by an altar tombstone in the churchyard of Bendochy. Patrick, fourth son of George Roger, born March 1693, rented a farm at Coupar-Grange. He married, 14th August 1718, Margaret Kidd, parish of St Martins, and had issue six sons, James, George, William, Thomas, Charles, and Patrick, and four daughters, Janet, Jean, Barbara, and Margaret. Janet, eldest daughter, born January 1727, married John Blair, and had issue. James, eldest son, born November 1719, married Margaret Corson, and had issue, Peter, born

September 1748; James, born April 1750; Margaret, born March 1752; and Sophia, born September 1754. George, second son, engaged in business at Dundee, married, and had issue. William, third son, rented a farm at Tealing, married, and had issue. Charles, fifth son, a manufacturer, and Convener of the Incorporated Trades in Dundee, married, first, Grizel, eldest daughter of Thomas Davidson, of Wolflaw, and secondly, Catherine Young, Dundee. By his second marriage he had issue, Charles Young Roger, a daughter Catherine, and others.

William, eldest son of George Roger, was baptized 20th January 1684. He married, first, Margaret Wright, daughter of the Laird of Lawton, near Coupar-Angus, and secondly (12th August 1726), Janet Gellatly, parish of Lethendy. By his first marriage he had issue, George, born May 1716; Jean, born January 1711; Janet, born June 1714; Barbara, born March 1718; and Sophia, born April 1719, who died young. By his second marriage, he had issue, William, born June 1727; Peter, born May 1732; David, born February 1735; and Sophia, born December 1729.

Of William Roger's daughters, Jean, the eldest, married her cousin, George Playfair, farmer, Knowhead; she died at St Andrews in 1804, aged ninety-three. She was mother of two sons, William and James. William, baptized 7th December 1736, died young. James, the younger son, born December 1738, was ordained minister of Newtyle, Forfarshire, 1st November 1770. He was translated to the neighouring parish of Meigle, and in 1799 was appointed Principal of the United College, St Andrews, and minister of St Leonard's Church in that city. Principal Playfair published " Systems of Chronology and Geography," and other historical works. He was Doctor of Divinity, and Historiographer to His Royal Highness the Prince of Wales. He died 26th May 1819. He married, 30th September 1773, Margaret Lyon * (descended

---

* Mrs Playfair's brother, the Rev. James Lyon, D.D., minister of Glammis (died 3d April 1838), married, 25th January 1786, Agnes, daughter of John Ramsay L'Amy, of Dunkenny, Forfarshire. This lady was author of " Neil Gow's

from a branch of the noble family of Strathmore), who died 4th November 1831, and had four sons and five daughters. George, the eldest son, born 1782, became Principal Inspector-General of Hospitals, Bengal. He married Jessie Ross, and had issue (with others now deceased), George, born 1816, lately Principal of the Medical College, Agra ; Lyon, a Privy Councillor, and M.P. for the Universities of St Andrews and Edinburgh ; Robert Lambert, born 1828, lately Consul at Zanzibar, and now Consul-General at Algiers ; William Smoult, born 1835, physician in London; and James Octavius, deceased. George Playfair died in 1845.

The Right Honourable Lyon Playfair, C.B., second son of Dr George Playfair, was born at Bengal in 1818. In 1843 he was appointed Professor of Chemistry in the Royal Institution, Manchester. After serving as a Sanitary Commissioner, Chemist to the Museum of Practical Geology, Joint Secretary to the Department of Science and Art, and Inspector-General of Government Museums, he was in 1858 elected Professor of Chemistry in the University of Edinburgh, and President of the Chemical Society of London. He resigned his university chair in 1869, on being elected representative in Parliament of the Universities of St Andrews and Edinburgh. He is Ph.D. of Giessen, LL.D. of St Andrews and Edinburgh, a Fellow of the Royal Society, and Companion of the Bath. Dr Lyon Playfair married, in 1846, Margaret, daughter of James Oakes, of Riddings, Derbyshire ; and in 1857, Jean Ann, daughter of Crowley Millington, of Crowley House, and has issue.

William Davidson Playfair, second son of Principal Playfair, and grandson of Jean Roger, born 1783, became a Colonel in the Indian Army; he married Ann Ross, and had issue thirteen sons and daughters, of whom survive *Colonel* George William, *Major* Elliot Minto, *Major* William, and Jessie, wife of Stuart Grace, town-clerk, St Andrews. Colonel W. D. Playfair died in 1852.

Lieutenant-Colonel Sir Hugh Lyon Playfair, LL.D., third

Farewell to Whisky," and other poetical compositions. She died 14th December 1840.

son of Principal Playfair, was born in 1786. He was distinguished in India as an artillery officer, and as constructor of the great military road between Calcutta and Benares. For many years chief magistrate of St Andrews, he found the place in decay, and effected its restoration. For his important services in India, and as restorer of the city of St Andrews, he was honoured with knighthood and other distinctions. He died at St Andrews on the 23d January 1861, in the 75th year of his age. He is commemorated by an elegant monument in the cathedral churchyard, St Andrews. By his marriage with Jane Dalgleish, of Scotscraig, he had eleven children. His eldest son, William Dalgleish, lieutenant in the 33d Regiment, Bengal Native Infantry, fell at the battle of Sobraon, 16th February 1846, aged 25 years. His second son, Arthur, an officer in the Indian Army, also fell in one of the engagements in India. Frederick, third son, now a major in the Indian Army, married in 1855, and has issue. Archibald, fourth son, is in the Indian service. The youngest son, Henry, is resident in Glasgow. Of Sir Hugh's daughters, Margaret Adelaide, the eldest, married *Lieutenant* Charles M'Kechnie, 93d Regiment, and died, leaving issue. Jane Julia, second daughter, is wife of Gregor M'Gregor, banker, St Andrews. Mary, third daughter, married Charles Murray, merchant, China; and Frances Makgill, fourth daughter, married William Lees, A.M.

James Playfair, youngest son of Principal Playfair, and grandson of Jean Roger, was born in 1791. He was a merchant in Glasgow, and a magistrate of that city. He was twice married, and left issue. His eldest surviving son, John, is settled as a merchant in Toronto. Another son, George, is a merchant at Glasgow. His only daughter, Margaret, is wife of the Rev. William Fraser, A.M., minister of Free St Bernard's Church, Edinburgh. James Playfair died in 1866.

Of Principal Playfair's five daughters, Margaret, the eldest, died unmarried, August 1810. Jean, second daughter, married Patrick Playfair, of Dalmarnock, 4th February 1802. Janet, third daughter, married the Rev. James Macdonald; she died 20th October 1864. Mary Lyon, fourth daughter, married, 14th May 1808, Colonel (afterwards General) David Campbell, of Williamston, Perthshire ; she died in 1810, leaving one son, James David Lyon Campbell, of Williamston, who married Alicia Richarda Houghton, and had issue, four sons, Charles, Henry, George, and Arthur. The Principal's youngest daughter, Hugh Elizabeth, married, 23d January 1810, Samuel Caw, merchant, Glasgow ; issue, two sons, John, deceased, and James, an eminent artist.

Barbara, third daughter of William Roger, married James Millar, farmer, Coupar-Grange, and had issue, one son, George, who died *s. p.*, and four daughters, Isabella, married William Taylor, Meigle ; Jean, married John Duncan, farmer, Bothrie, died *s. p.* ; Elizabeth, married Peter Crichton, farmer, Hatton, parish of Newtyle, with issue ; and Barbara, married William Gow, farmer, Coupar-Grange, with issue.

Sophia, fifth daughter of William Roger, born 1729, married, 23d August 1751, John Playfair, farmer, West Town of Coupar-Grange, and had issue, four sons, William, born February 1755 (died young) ; John, born 1763 ; Patrick, born September 1765 ; James, born March 1769 (died young) ; and four daughters, Anne, born February 1753 ; Sophia, born January 1762 (died young) ; Jean, born July 1767 ; and Margaret, born April 1771. Anne, the eldest daughter, married, 20th December 1774, Thomas Myles, merchant, Perth, and had issue, three sons, John, Robert, and Thomas. The two latter died unmarried. John engaged in merchandise. He married Margaret, daughter of the Rev. Alexander Blyth, minister of the Associate Church, Kinclaven, Perthshire, and had issue. His eldest son, the Rev. Thomas Myles, minister of Aberlemno, Forfarshire, is author of "The Kernel of the Controversy," and other publications. John, a younger son, is a solicitor in Forfar. Jean, third daughter of John Playfair and Sophia Roger, married Peter Grant, Perth, and had children, who all died young. Margaret, youngest daughter of John Playfair, married Robert Davidson, farmer, Tealing, Forfarshire, and left one daughter, who married Thomas Mudie, and had issue.

John, second son of John Playfair and Sophia Roger, married Margaret Henderson. He was a merchant in Perth, and there died in 1833 without issue.

Patrick, third son of John Playfair and Sophia Roger, engaged in merchandise in Antigua, and having realised a fortune, purchased the estate of Dalmarnock, in the county of Lanark. He married, 4th February 1802, Jean, second daughter of Principal James Playfair, of St Andrews; she died 24th November 1852. Patrick Playfair died 26th November 1836; he was father of five sons and five daughters. James, the eldest son, died, unmarried, 22d February 1866; two sons, each named John, died young; Patrick is a merchant in Glasgow, and President of the Chamber of Commerce in that city; he married Georgiana, daughter of John Muir, merchant, Glasgow, and has issue, six sons and three daughters; the youngest son is the Rev. David Playfair, B.A., Cantab., minister of Abercorn, Linlithgowshire; he married, in 1854, Jane Kincaid, daughter of James Pitcairn, M.D., Edinburgh, and has issue two sons and two daughters.

Margaret, eldest daughter of Patrick Playfair, and granddaughter of Sophia Roger, married, 27th April 1831, the Rev. Charles Jobson Lyon, minister of the Episcopal Church, St Andrews, and author of "History of St Andrews," 2 vols., 8vo, Edin., 1843—and has issue, three sons and two daughters. Sophia, second daughter of Patrick Playfair, married, 1st October 1834, the Rev. James Chrystal, D.D., minister of Auchinleck, with issue, four sons and two daughters. Mary, third daughter of Patrick Playfair, and granddaughter of Sophia Roger, married, 23d July 1839, the Rev. Patrick Fairbairn, D.D., Principal of the Free Church College, Glasgow; she died 9th December 1852, leaving two sons and two daughters. Anne and Jane Hugh, younger daughters of Patrick Playfair of Dalmarnock, are unmarried.

George Roger, son of William Roger by his first wife, Margaret Wright, died unmarried; William, second son of

William Roger, and first by his second marriage, rented the farm of Coupar-Grange. He married, first, Isabella, daughter of George Constable, Bendochy, and secondly, Elizabeth, daughter of J. Robertson, Tullinydie. His two sons George and William, and his daughter Margaret, died in infancy. His surviving daughter Janet married John West, farmer, Mayriggs, parish of Bendochy, and had issue, two sons.

Peter, third son of William Roger, rented the farm of Ryehill, Coupar-Grange. On the 27th June 1766, he married Janet, youngest daughter of Thomas Davidson, of Wolflaw, parish of Oathlaw, Forfarshire. This gentleman was born in 1705 ; he married Anne Curr, by whom he had one son and three daughters. Grizel, the eldest daughter, married, first, James Davidson, shipmaster, Dundee ; and secondly, Charles Roger, manufacturer, Dundee (see *supra*). Margaret, the second daughter, was born in 1731, and married James Neish, merchant, Dundee ; she died in 1824, leaving three sons and two daughters. The family of Neish is represented by James Neish, of Laws and Omachie, and William Neish, of Clepington and Tannadice, grandsons of Mrs Margaret Neish or Davidson.

John, only son of Thomas Davidson, of Wolflaw, was born in 1747 ; he succeeded to his father's inheritance, and died unmarried in 1779, when the property was sold. Thomas Davidson was only child of Alexander Davidson, Baldragon, parish of Auchterhouse, Forfarshire, and of his wife, Margaret Fleming. The family were cadets of the House of Davidson of Balgay.

Peter Roger, and his wife, Janet Davidson, had three sons, James and Charles, of whom hereafter, and John, born 29th March 1772, who died in 1780 ; and four daughters, Anne, born July 1769, died in 1780 ; Margaret, born 17th July 1774, died 24th November 1858 ; Sophia, a twin with her brother Charles, born 5th November 1780, died 7th May 1822 ; and Isabella, born 21st April 1777, died 23d December 1854. Peter Roger died 27th January 1809, and his wife, Janet Davidson, 23d June 1825.

Charles, younger son of Peter Roger and Janet Davidson, was born 5th November 1780, and died 26th March 1865. In 1847 he published a work entitled "A Collation of the Sacred Scriptures," in which the more remarkable variations in the several English versions have been ingeniously compared. He married, first, in 1810, Isabella Allan; secondly, in September 1817, Anne Cruikshank; and thirdly, in 1828, Jane Mac-Laggan; and had issue, by his second marriage, three sons, Charles, James, and Patrick, and a daughter, Anne; and by his third marriage, Sarah, and Sophia. Charles, the eldest son, published "The Rise of Canada," Quebec, 1856, 8vo. James Cruikshank, the second son, is a barrister-at-law; he has contributed to the periodicals some interesting papers on heraldry and Scottish antiquities.

James, eldest son of Peter Roger, was born on the 24th June 1767. Having studied at the Universities of St Andrews and Aberdeen, he obtained license as a probationer of the Established Church on the 4th May 1791. He was ordained minister of Dunino, in the county of Fife, on the 2d May, 1805, and died 23d November 1849. He published "General View of the Agriculture of Angus, with Preliminary Observations, by George Dempster, Esq. of Dunnichen," Edin., 1794, 4to, and "Essay on Government," Edin., 1797, 8vo; he contributed to the Old and New Statistical Accounts of Scotland.* He married Jane, daughter of the Rev. William Haldane, minister of Kingoldrum, and granddaughter of James Haldane of Bermony. This branch of an old Scottish House claims particular notice.

Of Norse origin, the family name of Haldane has long been common in Denmark. Haldenus, a Danish chief, obtained lands in the parish of Sprouston, Roxburghshire, which were called after him. In the twelfth century, a younger son of Haldane of that ilk married the heiress of Gleneagles in Perthshire. A charter of the lands of Frandie, forming part of the Gleneagles estate, was granted to Roger de Halden

---

* For Recollections of the Rev. James Roger of Dunino, see "A Century of Scottish Life," Edin., 1871, 12mo., pp. 40-97.

by King William the Lion (Sir James Dalrymple's Collections, p. 392). Aylmer de Haldane, of Gleneagles, was one of the barons who, in 1296, swore fealty to Edward I. Sir John Haldane, of Gleneagles, after holding various important offices, was, in the reign of James III., appointed Justice-General of Scotland, beyond the Forth; he died in 1493. His grandson, Sir John Haldane, fell at Flodden. The next Laird of Gleneagles was one of the Lords of the Congregation. The family was during the present century represented by the brothers, Robert Haldane of Airthrey, and Captain James Alexander Haldane, both so remarkable for their missionary zeal and religious earnestness.

The lands of Easter Keillor, in the parish of Newtyle, Forfarshire, belonged at the commencement of the sixteenth century to Sylvester Halden or Haldane. He in 1514 witnessed a *retour* confirming Alexander Lindsay in the office of hereditary blacksmith of the lordship of Brechin.* In 1574 George Halden was reader at the church of Newtyle, with a salary of £20 Scots.† In 1645 Easter Keillor fell to Susan, heiress of her brother, Alexander Haldane.‡ The estate afterwards passed from the family of Haldane to Halyburton of Pitcur;§ it is now included in the Wharncliffe estates. Another branch of the Haldane family were owners of Bermony, parish of Alyth, Perthshire. According to tradition, the lands of Bermony were granted to the Haldanes by James V., who, on visiting the locality in disguise, received some act of kindness from "the gudewife." The tenure was celebrated in the following rhyme:

> " Ye Haddens o' the Moor ye pay nocht,
> But a harren tether if its socht,
> A red rose at Yule, and a sna' ba' at Lammas."

—— Haldane, Laird of Bermony, in the beginning of the eighteenth century, married —— Donaldson, sister of the Rev.

* Spalding Club Miscellany, vol. v., p. 292.
† Register of Ministers and Readers, 1574. Miscellany of Wodrow Society, vol. i., p. 355.
‡ Inq. Spec., Forfar, No. 288.   § Jervise's Angus and Mearns, p. 321.

C

James Donaldson, minister of Glammis, whose only child, Jean Donaldson, married, 15th August 1770, James Hay of Seggieden, Perthshire ; the present proprietor of Seggieden, Mrs Drummond Hay, is her granddaughter. Of the marriage of —— Haldane of Bermony and his wife, —— Donaldson, were born a son, James, and two daughters.

Barbara, elder daughter, married, August 1726, the Rev. Thomas Aytone, minister of Alyth, and had a daughter, Marjorie.* Mr Aytone married, secondly, Margaret, daughter of Principal Hadow of St Andrews. A native of Roxburghshire, he was ordained minister of Alyth in 1720; he was translated to Kilconquhar, Fifeshire, in 1735, and died 5th January 1739, aged forty-five. Elizabeth, younger daughter, married, June 1727, James Brown, Alyth, Perthshire. Of this marriage were born three sons, David, Andrew, and John. John, the youngest son, married his cousin Margaret, daughter of James Haldane of Bermony, and had two sons, James and William, and a daughter, Jean, who died unmarried. James, the elder son, married, without issue. William, the second son, proceeded in 1820 to the United States of America. He married Margaret Hain, of the village of Ceres, Fifeshire, and had three sons, John, James, and Thomas, and two daughters, Jean and Margaret. John, the eldest son, has a son, William, a minister of the Presbyterian Church, United States ; James, the second son, is a D.D., and minister of the Presbyterian Church, Keokuk, Iowa ; Thomas, the youngest son, is minister of the Presbyterian Church, Crawfordville, Iowa.

James Haldane succeeded his father in the estate of Bermony. He married Christian, daughter of William Mackintosh, Muirton, Perthshire, and had a son, William, and two daughters, Margaret and Jean. Margaret, elder daughter, was born 11th August 1750; she married her cousin, John Brown (see *supra*), with issue. Jean, younger daughter, born 7th April 1765, married —— Mill, and had a daughter, Anne, now Mrs Mackintosh.

* Parish Register of Alyth.

William, only son of James Haldane of Bermony, was born in 1762. Having studied at the University of St Andrews, he obtained license as a probationer of the Established Church on the 18th June 1788. He was ordained minister of Glenisla, Forfarshire, on the 7th April 1795, and was translated to the parish of Kingoldrum, in the same county, on the 20th April 1803. He died 27th May 1836. The Rev. William Haldane married, 17th May 1796, Anne, second daughter of the Rev. Charles Roberts ; she died 18th September 1846.

The Rev. Charles Roberts descended from a family of yeomen, named Robert, long connected with the county of Kincardine. His father, Alexander Robert, rented the Mains of Phesdo, a considerable farm, in the lease of which he succeeded his father, who bore the same Christian name.* Charles Roberts was born in the parish of Fordoun, Kincardineshire, in May 1727. He was some time incumbent of the Episcopal Church, Dundee, and died about his 45th year, during a visit to Antigua. He married, about 1758, Anne, elder daughter of Sir John Ogilvy, Bart. of Inverquharity, by his first wife, Anne, eldest daughter of James Carnegie, of Finhaven.

David Carnegie, second Earl of Northesk, provided, in 1672, the lands of Finhaven to his second son, James. These lands were erected into a barony in 1676. The Hon. James Carnegie, of Finhaven, married, in 1674, Anna, second daughter of Robert Maitland, brother of John, Duke of Lauderdale, and his wife, Dame Margaret Lundin, of that ilk ; she died 3d September 1694. Of this marriage were born two sons and two daughters. Margaret, elder daughter, married the Hon. Patrick Lyon, of Auchterhouse, and died 14th April 1742 ; Jean, second daughter, married her cousin, Alexander Blair, of Kinfauns, who assumed the name of Carnegie ; Charles, the elder son, died unmarried ; James, the second son, succeeded his father in 1707 in the barony of Finhaven. In resenting an insult by the Earl of Strathmore, he inadvertently killed that nobleman, an act for which he was tried, and ac-

* Registers of Fordoun parish.

quitted. He died in 1765. By his first wife, Margaret, daughter of Sir William Bennet, of Grubbet, he had two daughters, Anne and Margaret. The former, as already stated, was first wife of Sir John Ogilvy, Bart. of Inverquharity (Fraser's Earls of Southesk, p. 425).

Of the marriage of the Rev. Charles Roberts and Anne, elder daughter of Sir John Ogilvy, Bart., and his wife, Anne Carnegie, of Finhaven, were born two daughters. Mary, the younger daughter, married, 28th April 1792, the Rev. Thomas Ogilvy, minister of Kirriemuir, with issue. Anne, the elder daughter, was wife of the Rev. William Haldane.

Anne Ogilvy or Roberts married, secondly, John Duff, Esq., of the family of Duff of Braco, Banffshire, ancestors of the Earls of Fife. Of this marriage were born two sons and three daughters. Both the sons held commissions in the army, and fell at Seringapatam. Barbara and Margaret, the second and third daughters, died unmarried. Innes, the eldest daughter, became second wife of the Rev. John Skinner, Dean of Dunkeld, author of "Annals of Scottish Episcopacy," son of Bishop John Skinner, of Aberdeen, and grandson of the Rev. John Skinner, author of "Tullochgorum." Dean Skinner was born 20th August 1769, and died 2d September 1841. His widow, Mrs Innes Skinner, died in April 1872, aged ninety-four.

Of the marriage of the Rev. William Haldane and Anne Roberts, were born five sons and three daughters. Two sons, William and Thomas, and two daughters, Innes and Anne, died young and unmarried. John, the eldest son, was a physician in London ; he married, but died *s.p.* Walter, the second son, born in 1802, was a merchant in Dundee ; he died in 1838, aged 36. He married Susan, daughter of Charles Hill, Forfar, and had one son, William, who died in infancy, and two daughters. Margaret, the elder daughter, is unmarried. Anne Stirling, the younger daughter, married, 6th August 1863, Nicholson, second son of the Rev. John Cumming, D.D., F.R.S.E., minister of the Scots Church, Crown Court, Covent Garden London, author of "Apocalyptic Sketches," and other works.

Of this marriage are born two sons, Walter John Haldane, and William Haldane.

James Ogilvy Haldane, fourth son of the Rev. William Haldane and Anne Roberts, was licensed as a probationer of the Scottish Church, 3d October 1832. He was, on the 20th October 1836, ordained minister of Kingoldrum, in succession to his father. He married, 23d November 1871, Helen Gunn, of Caithness-shire.

Jane, second daughter of the Rev. William Haldane and Anne Roberts, born 19th January 1804, married, 23d January 1823 (see *supra*), the Rev. James Roger, minister of Dunino ; she died 18th April 1825, leaving an only child, Charles Rogers—born same day—the author of these memoirs.

A branch of the Roxburghshire family of Roger, which early settled on lands belonging to Dryburgh Abbey, at Crail, Fifeshire, long enjoyed considerable affluence, and is still represented in that district. Of a branch which settled at Edinburgh prior to the Reformation, one household seems after that event to have clung to the old faith, for in October 1563, Christian Pynkertoun, wife of James Roger, merchant-burgess in Edinburgh, was arraigned before the Justiciary Court for being present at mass in Holyrood Chapel.* John Roger, of the Canongate, Edinburgh, conformed to Protestantism ; on the 2d December, 1564, he had his "maiden child Dorothy" baptized by the minister of the Canongate.†

Members of the Roger family at Ochiltree spread over Ayrshire. On the 18th November 1507, Mr Martin Rede, chancellor of the diocese of Glasgow, apprenticed Thomas Roger to a burgess of Irvine. ‡ Alexander Roger was witness to a legal instrument, dated at Dundonald, 28th November 1510, by which the prior and convent of the Preaching Friars at Ayr leased certain lands in the parish of Symington.§

A descendant of the Ochiltree family, William Roger, settled in Ayr as a merchant, and became prosperous. Dying

* Pitcairn's Criminal Trials.   † Baptismal Register of the Canongate.
‡ Diocesan Reg. of Glasgow.   Printed for the Grampian Club, vol. i., p. 400.
§ *Ib.*, vol. ii., p. 383.

in January 1578, he was succeeded by his brother, Thomas Roger.* A son of Thomas was parliamentary commissioner for the burgh of Ayr; his name as "Wilelmus Roger, pro Air," appears on the roll of the Parliament held in Holyrood House on the 28th January 1593. He was father of the Rev. Ralph Roger, an eminent sufferer in the cause of Presbytery. Ralph Roger was ordained minister of Ardrossan on the 27th May 1647. Declining a call to Ayr, his native parish, he was afterwards preferred, on the invitation of the people, to the Cathedral Church, Glasgow. To this charge he was admitted on the 5th June 1659. Having joined the protesting party he was, in October 1662, deprived of his charge. By the Privy Council, on the 7th June 1669, he was "indulged" at Kilwinning, being the first who was so favoured. He was one of those who, on the 14th December 1670, met at Paisley with Archbishop Leighton, with a view to an accommodation. For not observing the anniversary of the Restoration, he was fined in half his stipend, 8th July 1673. In the year 1676 he preached in Glasgow. In the year following he presided at a meeting of "outed" Presbyterian ministers, attended both by the indulged and non-indulged. On the removal of the indulgence in 1684, he was imprisoned at Edinburgh, for refusing "to give bond not to exercise his ministry in any part of Scotland." On the renewal of the indulgence in 1687 he resumed his ministrations at Glasgow. Mr Ralph Roger died on the 3d February 1689. He married, first, Margaret, daughter of Alexander Wryttowne, in Kilwinning, and secondly, Janet Craigengelt. In his personal estate he was succeeded by his only daughter Maria.†

A member of the Ochiltree family obtained in 1599 the lands of Wester Rossland, Renfrewshire.‡ His descendants acquired the adjacent lands of Hay-hill, Long-Meadows, and Gladstone, all formerly belonging to the Brisbanes of Bishop-

---

* Will of William Roger, merchant-burgess in Ayr, confirmed 26th September 1598 (Edinburgh Commissariat Register).

† Fasti Eccl. Scot, vol. ii., pp. 5, 6, 157, 181.

‡ In the Act of Exceptions from the Act of Indemnity, passed in 1662, John Roger, of Park, Renfrewshire, is fined £300 Scots.

town. The Rev. Mathew Rodger, minister of the College Church, St Andrews, is the present proprietor of Rossland, and is the representative of this branch.

A branch of the Ochiltree family settled at Glasgow,* and there obtained considerable opulence.† In the Rental Book of the Diocese of Glasgow is the following entry: "The xxix of Januer, 1570, Gabriel Roger is rentellit in viii^s· & xj^d· land in Mayrhill [Maryhill, near Glasgow] be consent of Thomas Dawe," etc. William Rodger was a prosperous merchant in Glasgow in 1605.‡ Of that city, Robert Rodger, his grandson, was Dean of Guild in 1698 ; he subsequently became Lord Provost, and in 1708 was elected M.P. for the burghs of Glasgow, Renfrew, Dumbarton, and Rutherglen. His son Hugh also held the office of Lord Provost.§ Robert Rodger, son of William Rodger, merchant, Glasgow, and a magistrate of the city, contributed to the Maitland Club a quarto volume, edited by Mr Joseph Stevenson, entitled, "Documents illustrative of Sir William Wallace, his Life and Times." His sister, Janet Rodger, married, in 1829, General Sir John Alexander Agnew Wallace, Bart. of Lochryan, and is mother of Sir William Wallace, Bart., now of Lochryan.

Of the House of Roger of Ochiltree, a branch settled in Ireland. On the 11th May 1613,‖ John Roger obtained the farm of Dryan, in the barony of Raphoe, and county of Donegal, from James Cunningham of Glengarnock, an Ayrshire landowner, who, three years before, had acquired forfeited lands in Ulster. In effecting a settlement in Ireland, John Roger may have been assisted by James, Lord Ochiltree, who interested himself in the settlement of Ulster.¶ In Ireland members of the family occupy a respectable status ;

---

* In Lib. Coll. Nostri Domine, Robert Roger and William Roger occur as owners of property at Glasgow in the first half of the 16th century.

† Diocesan Reg. of Glasgow, vol. i., p. 191.

‡ View of the Merchants' House of Glasgow.   Glasgow, 1856, 4to, p. 91.

§ Anderson's Scottish Nation, *voce* Roger.

‖ Inq. Canc. Hib. Rep. ii.

¶ Correspondence of the Earl of Melrose, 4to, vol. i., p. 172.

several are ministers of the Irish Presbyterian Church. There is a place called Rogerstown in the county of Louth.

The armorial escutcheon of the Scottish House of Roger has not been satisfactorily determined. Quoting from Workman's MS., Nisbet assigns Roger, "of that ilk," vert on a fesse argent between three piles in chief, and a cinquefoil in base of the last—a saltier of the first. " Mr Pont," he adds, "gives to the name of Roger only vert a fesse argent, and to another family of the name, sable, a stag's head erased argent, holding in its mouth a mullet *or*." * The members of the Scottish House have spelt the name variously—such as Roger, Rogers, Rodger, and Rodgers. The Coupar-Grange branch long maintained the original spelling, but the present representative has adopted the English form.

These Memorials were incomplete without some reference to an eminent person of the name, who shares with James I. the honour of originating Scottish music. Sir William Roger was introduced to the court of James III., in the train of the ambassador of Edward IV. His musical abilities recommended him to the king, who appointed him president of the school of music, and in guerdon of his services granted him knighthood, and raised him to the Privy Council. To enable him to sustain his rank, the king, by a charter under the Great Seal, dated 29th November 1469, bestowed on him the lands of Traquair, forfeited by Lord Boyd. † The elevation of Roger and of others, whom the king, on account of their accomplishments, delighted to honour, exasperated the nobility, who menaced vengeance. To modify their resentment, Roger, after possessing the lands of Traquair for nine years, disposed of them at a nominal sum to the Earl of Buchan, one of the most powerful and vigorous of his opponents. On the 19th September 1478, he executed a notarial instrument of sale in favour of Lord Buchan, disposing of his entire estate for seventy merks Scots, or £3, 15s. 10d. sterling. But the

---

* Nisbet's Heraldry, vol. i., pp. 59.

† Traquair Papers, quoted in Chambers's History of Peeblesshire, Edin., 1864, 8vo, pp. 81-86.

self-denial of the musician did not avail in subduing the animosity cherished against him and the king's other favourites. In 1482, when the king was on an expedition southward to check the advance of an English army, Lord Buchan and other nobles seized on the royal favourites, and without legal form condemned them to execution. Sir William Roger was, with others, hanged at the Bridge of Lauder. " Roger's musical compositions," remarks Mr Tytler,* "were fitted to refine and improve the barbarous taste of the age, and his works were long after highly esteemed in Scotland." †

* History of Scotland, by Patrick Fraser Tytler. Edin., 1869, 12mo, vol. ii., p. 243.

† Several seals associated with the name of Sir William Roger in Mr Henry Laing's Supplementary Catalogue of Scottish Seals (1866, 4to), are modern forgeries (Notes and Queries, 1868-71, *passim*).

INDEX.

McFarlane & Erskine, Printers, Edinburgh.

www.ingramcontent.com/pod-product-compliance
Lightning Source LLC
Chambersburg PA
CBHW030910260626

47169CB00008B/2781